1

Savanna Therapeutic Stories
savanna-therapeutic.org.uk

Written by Talya Bruck and Dr Gail Sinitsky
Guest illustrated by Paul Banks

ISBN: 9798861804462

First Edition

Summary: *Here We Go Again! – A Story About Bullying* highlights the importance of seeking help at a difficult time. Bullying can be a complicated and painful experience, and sadly something that many children struggle with. The story aims to help children find their voices and shines a light on the power of kindness and compassion. In the story, Peter the panther is being bullied by Robbie the meerkat. He finds it hard to let others know what is happening but his friend Hetty the hedgehog is there to encourage him to seek help. Read on to find out how Peter finds his voice.

Dedication

Bullying is a well-known, painful and complex difficulty that many children and adults have had to face. Our book is dedicated to everyone who has survived, with courage, integrity and inspiration.

"I've learned that people will forget what you said, people will forget what you did, but they will never forget how you made them feel ."
Maya Angelou

Acknowledgements

Writing a story about bullying was a somewhat tricky task as we endeavored to understand the subject from all perspectives and positions, whilst maintaining utmost focus on those who are subject to such unkindness.

As always, there are kind and generous people who have offered their support to ensure that the book works. We would like to extend thanks to all these people. We would also like to thank all the children, young people, and families who we have been privileged to work with over the years: you have enriched us with wisdom which we draw upon when writing.

We would also like to thank Leo, Talia, Isabella, Bee, Luna, Rowena, Matilda, Solomon and Karen for reviewing the book.

A special thanks and credit to the following for their photography which has inspired some of the *Savanna Therapeutic Stories* landscapes: Dr Peter James Chisholm, Thomas Fuhrmann and CT Cooper.

As always, our deep gratitude goes to Philippe Miguet for his meticulous design and technical support, without which this book would not have been possible.

Foreword

Do you remember when you were little? So many new things to experience, some overwhelming or scary, others exciting. Friendships, too, were a big learning curve. When you are at school friendship is vital in order to feel happy, but at times it is so hard for children to navigate relationships with peers. For example, knowing whether what your friend is doing is or isn't ok. It can be really confusing for children when their friends or their classmates are doing things which don't feel right or good, like saying or doing mean things, and it's so tricky for children to know when these behaviours are bullying.

Bullying can be harmful for a child and leads to long lasting emotional and mental health problems. This is why we need to help them find their words to talk about these things as they begin to happen and not try to cope with it themselves, like so many children do. Trying to explain bullying to a young child can be difficult, finding the right words to help them understand.

When difficult experiences and feelings aren't talked about, they stay trapped within our children and come out in other ways, for example through mood, or getting more angry than normal or sadder, or in behaviours like becoming withdrawn or clingy. Children do not have the inner resources to understand and process what is going on. They need help to talk, to feel their feelings and to have adults make sure they are safe.

That's exactly why we need stories like Here we go again! - A story about bullying, written by Talya Bruck and Dr Gail Sinitsky. Highly skilled and experienced child clinicians, they have created a story which is highly relatable for little ones. In the story, Peter the panther and his friends address the difficult time Peter is having at school when two other classmates begin to turn on him.

Here We Go Again! - A Story About Bullying uses simple words and lovely illustrations to help a child think about their feelings through the story and start to understand what has been going on for them. Reading this story with your child will help them and you to have conversations around bullying and the more you talk openly to your children about bullying, the more comfortable they will be telling you if they see or experience it in the future.

Sara Anton
Child, Adolescent and Family Psychotherapist
saraanton.com

A note for Parents/Educators and Therapists

Telling and listening to stories has long been humankind's way of processing and making sense of the world. It is also a way to understand how we interact as humans and to recognise our unique differences that are to be celebrated.

By using stories as metaphors, *Savanna Therapeutic Stories* endeavors to support children, young people, and their families to comprehend the differences in us all and to identify what makes each of us unique.

We believe that encouraging meaningful conversations through story is a key responsibility of the adults in children and young people's lives. Helping children and young people to express and explore how they feel through the use of curious, gentle questions enables them to process their thoughts and experiences in a nurturing way.

Stories can also help children and young people to better understand themselves, other people, and the world around them.

Here We Go Again! – A Story About Bullying focuses on a topic that unfortunately is still all too common in our society.

It can raise complicated and uncomfortable feelings in us. Unless addressed, bullying can sadly have lasting effects which can be taken into adulthood. By opening up conversations about this topic, our story contributes to raising awareness and making a difference. Our best hope is that our story helps children and young people to recognise that bullying is not something they should accept or endure, but that they can use their voices to seek help and make a change.

Warm wishes,

Talya & Gail

Reflections on Talking to Children and Young People

Talking about bullying can be tricky. It not only links to our own past experiences of how we might have talked or not talked in our families of origin but is also connected to how we process our emotions today. This can understandably raise anxiety. However, as adults, it is our role to help children notice and appreciate differences, make sense of their worlds, and develop healthy emotional regulation. Helpful, gentle and open conversations are a key part of this process.

▶ When reading this story with a child or young person, it can be helpful to acknowledge and share how you have each understood the story. It can be useful to discuss or highlight any different perspectives in understanding the same character or storyline.

▶ When discussing the story, it is important to explicitly name the themes raised in the book. This not only gives children and young people a shared language to use but also importantly gives them permission to talk about what is sometimes unnamed and difficult to communicate.

▶ Telling the story in an expressive manner can help with exploring emotions. This could be particularly helpful for children and young people who may experience difficulties in identifying and expressing feelings. You could even develop this further by using puppets and/or encouraging children and young people to create their own endings to the story.

► Where possible, try to remain in a position of curiosity during your conversations. It can be tempting to try to 'fix' a child's problem by giving lots of advice, but the process of listening and validating a child's experience, as well as asking exploratory questions, helps children to talk openly without the fear of being judged or rescued. It can also really help to develop their communication and problem-solving skills.

► Normalising children's experiences of difficulties and hardship can be reassuring for children who feel alone and at times ashamed about the challenges they face in their daily lives.

It was another busy day at Bushlands Primary School on the Savanna.

The animals were talking and laughing with their friends, as they flooded through the school gates excitedly and entered their classrooms.

Peter the panther, Hetty the hedgehog, Silo the lion cub and Gerry the giraffe were the best of friends and they felt so lucky to be in the same class together.

As they walked in, heads down deep in conversation, Robbie the meerkat pushed Peter, causing him to drop his lunch.

Peter looked up as he collected his lunch from the floor and saw Robbie giggle with his friend, Margot the rhino. Peter held back his tears and thought to himself, '*Oh no, here we go again*' as he remembered the other times that Robbie had been unkind to him.

Later that same day at lunchtime, the little ones were playing their favourite game of football, cheering each other on.

Suddenly, the game sped up! Peter had the ball and was just about to deliver his super skilful kick when Robbie stuck out his foot and purposely tripped him up.

With a big crash, Peter fell to the floor.

Feeling dazed and hurt, he looked up just as his friends rushed over to check if he was okay. In the distance, he spotted Robbie and Margot fleeing to the other side of the playground in fits of laughter.

That night, Peter felt sad.

He told his mum he had a tummy ache and wasn't hungry, and he went to bed early. Tucked beneath his duvet, he thought back on the day with silent tears rolling down his cheeks.

He didn't want his mum to know he was upset - he just wished Robbie would stop!

The following day dawned bright and sunny.

Dragging his feet, Peter made his way to school, excited to see his friends, but scared about what Robbie would do next.

As he was walking through the school gates he heard Robbie behind him, so he quickened his pace to join Silo.

Later in their maths lesson, the teacher announced, "We will now be having a surprise maths quiz!" Robbie giggled and leant forward to whisper in Peter's ear: "You're so stupid, you won't even get one answer right!"

Peter turned around and wanted to shout, "*Stop it!*" but he felt himself shrinking back into his chair when Robbie stared him straight in the eye.

Hetty the hedgehog had overheard Robbie's unkind words. She was shocked and shouted, "Robbie, that's mean!" Robbie gulped and looked embarrassed.

After school, when the friends were walking home together, Hetty pulled Peter back and asked him, "Peter, what's going on with Robbie?"

Peter let a tear fall. Although he hadn't planned to tell her, it all came quickly gushing out. He told Hetty how Robbie had been so unkind to him for weeks.

Hetty was very sad to hear this and reached out to comfort Peter.

She rested her paw gently on his shoulder and said, "Oh how rude of him! That is bullying and it is so unfair. Have you told anyone about this?"

Peter shook his head sadly and whispered, "No, nobody. You're the only one I've told!"

Hetty thought about this for a moment and in a strong voice said, "I know what we need to do. We need to see El."

Now, El was the wise elephant of the Savanna who was always there to listen to the little ones. Every week, she would come into school to talk with them about anything they were worried about.

Hetty knew that El could help Peter, but Peter was worried. He looked at Hetty with big eyes and pleaded, "No, no, please! You can't tell anyone! If Robbie finds out I've told anyone, he will tease me more!"

Hetty replied, "But if you don't tell anyone, it might keep on happening and just look how bad you feel already."

With Hetty's help, Peter realised that he must speak to El, otherwise Robbie might not stop.

The next day at lunchtime, Hetty and Peter found El and asked if they could talk to her.

"Of course, little ones," she said in her kind and soft voice. "Let's go and find a quiet space."

They walked to the far end of the playground and sat together under the shade of the big baobab tree.

Gently, Hetty encouraged Peter to tell El what had been happening with Robbie. Peter spoke about the bullying with tears rolling down his face.

El listened carefully and nodded in encouragement until he finished.

"Oh Peter, this is very hurtful," said El. "It sounds like Robbie is bullying you."

"Really? Is it really bullying?" Peter exclaimed.

El carried on and said, "Yes - did you know that bullying is when someone does something intentionally to hurt you? It might be saying unkind things or even physically hurting you, like when Robbie tripped you up. It usually happens more than once and- "

"Well, this has been happening to poor Peter for weeks!" Hetty interrupted.

El, Peter and Hetty chatted together for some time, and after a while Peter let out a huge sigh of relief. "I'm so glad I told you! But what do we do now to stop it?"

Gently, El said, "I'm also so glad you told me. Hetty, you were a really good friend to Peter by encouraging him to do so."

Hetty and Peter smiled at each other, and then El continued, "You know, sometimes, when someone is having a tough time or feeling bad about themselves, they can end up being unkind to others. That's not okay. So, you've done the right thing by telling a grown up because now we can work out why it's happening and what to do next to help you."

El, Peter and Hetty set to work thinking through all the different things that might help Peter, including a plan to talk to his teacher.

That night, Peter told his mum everything that had been happening. His mum gave him a big hug and said, "I'm so pleased you told me."

"Well," Peter admitted, "I was afraid to tell anyone, but Hetty helped me to talk to El. We've come up with some ideas and my teacher is going to call you."

Peter's mum smiled and hugged him tightly again, and said, "Peter, I'm so proud of you! Asking for help is a very brave thing to do!"

That night, after a big dinner, Peter fell asleep warm beneath his duvet, feeling calm knowing that the adults around him were going to help.

Further note to Parents/Educators and Therapists

We hope that you find this story a helpful resource in facilitating curious and meaningful conversations about the themes of bullying highlighted in this book. Here are some ideas for questions to support your conversations:

► What did you think of this story?

► What do you think happened next at the end of the story? Write or draw your ideas for the ending you think would be best.

► Why do you think Peter didn't want his mum to know he was upset?

► How do you think Hetty helped Peter?

► Imagine if Robbie wrote Peter a letter of apology, what would he write?

► Have you ever found it hard to tell someone a problem you were having?

► Have you ever been bullied? Who or what helped you?

► Have you ever witnessed someone being bullied? What did you do? Or what could you do next time?

► Have you ever been unkind to someone? How did you make it right?

► Can you name something brave that you have done? Who noticed? What did they do or say?

Resources for Children, Young People and their Families

Organisations

▶ Youngminds
youngminds.org.uk

▶ Kidscape
kidscape.org.uk

▶ Childline
childline.org.uk

▶ Anti-Bullying Alliance
anti-bullyingalliance.org.uk

Children's and Young People's Books and Resources

▶ *Holly Hermit Crab's New Friends*
by Ann Graves, 2020

▶ *My Secret Bully*
by Trudy Ludwig, 2004

▶ *All About Feelings*
by Felicity Brooks & Frankie Allen, 2019

▶ *Will You Be My Friend?*
by Molly Potter, 2017

▶ *Kind*
by Axel Scheffler, 2020

▶ *Wonder*
by R J Palacio, 2014

▶ *The Night Bus Hero*
by Onjali Q Rauf, 2020

About Savanna Therapeutic Stories

Savanna Therapeutic Stories was established at the beginning of Covid-19 in 2020 in the call to offer support, understanding and meaning within an unprecedented time. The original stories aimed to help families, educators and therapists to support children and young people using metaphor to encourage conversation to explore feelings/emotions.

The original stories - *Hetty's in Lockdown, Things are Changing on the Savanna and The Returning* - were published digitally (PDF) in 2020 as a free resource to support young people. In 2021, Dramatherapist Patricia Ojehonmon and the author, Talya Bruck, also a Dramatherapist, updated the stories to reflect the changes in Covid-19.

These stories were: *Hetty's in Lockdown Again, The Changing Savanna and The Return.* All of these were published digitally (PDF). *Hetty's in Lockdown Again* is available as a narrated story on our YouTube channel *Therapeutic Tales*, narrated by Kadeem Tyrell and Patricia Ojehonmon with illustrations by Erin Cooper.

The stories tell the tale of four Savanna friends Silo, Peter, Hetty and Gerry along with El the wise elephant and how they navigate this tricky time. The stories explore the themes of change, the unknown, friendship, loss and much more.

Since this time, *Savanna Therapeutic Stories* has begun to explore other topics to help children and young people process difference, tricky feelings, and challenging situations and life experiences that they and their families might go through.

Other publications include:

Silo's Sadness written by Talya Bruck, illustrated by Erin Cooper, 2021

Talulah's Rules written by Talya Bruck, Dr Stella Mo and Rachel Ryan, illustrated by Erin Cooper, 2021

Tiana's Tale written by Talya Bruck and Patricia Ojehonmon, illustrated by Shaydon Tracey, 2021

Is It Me? written by Talya Bruck, illustrated by Jake Harris, 2022

Hugo's Hops written by Talya Bruck and Jessie Ellinor, illustrated by Paul Banks, 2022

Silo's Roar written by Talya Bruck and illustrated by Scarlett Altarace-Sherman, 2022

Authors

Talya Bruck is a Dramatherapist, Creative Arts Supervisor and Systemic Practitioner who works in CAMHS, has a private supervision practice, and works for OurTime helping to run a Kidstime workshop. She has over 20 years' experience working with children, young people, and families. She is passionate about supporting young people and their families to dream big and live the life they deserve.

She is the Founder of *Savanna Therapeutic Stories*. The stories, characters and setting are inspired by her past of being brought up in Africa as well as her many years of working with children, young people, and their families.

Dr Gail Sinitsky is a child and family Counselling Psychologist, passionate about and dedicated to promoting children's emotional and social well-being. She has worked in the field for over 15 years, across schools, charities and local child and adolescent mental health services (CAMHS).

She has a particular great love for designing and delivering therapeutic workshops and groups for children.

She founded Young & Mighty in 2020 (youngandmighty.com) with the realisation that there is still so much more that needs to be done to nurture positive mental health from a young age.

Gail was delighted to collaborate with Talya in the writing of this meaningful story about bullying.

Illustrator

Paul Banks is a qualified Aerospace Engineer who studied at Warwick University earning a Bachelor's Degree in Mechanical Engineering. His work has involved travel to many countries, and is currently based in North Carolina, USA. Alongside his professional career he explores his passion for art, graphic design, photography, cinematography and animation.

This is his second venture into illustration for *Savanna Therapeutic Stories*. He beautifully illustrated *Hugo's Hops* by Talya Bruck and Jessie Ellinor.

Printed in Great Britain
by Amazon

30250602R00030